THE
DIFFERENCE
MAKER

THE MINISTRIES OF THE BELIEVER

KINGSLEY LAWEND

CONTENTS

INTRODUCTION

Ministry isn't solely reserved for those within the fivefold ministry, nor is it confined to individuals with specific 'titles.' When someone experiences the new birth, they automatically step into ministry—the role of a difference-maker on earth, representing the Lord in every facet of life and within their sphere of influence. The duties of believers, God's saints, go beyond salvation and qualification for Heaven.

Upon embracing the new birth, each individual is entrusted with a unique ministry—the calling to be the light of the world, the salt of the earth, the fragrance of Christ, and God's battle-axe, among other roles. We're called to unveil the nature of our God across all aspects of life. Wherever a child of God finds themselves, they serve as the representative of heaven—an ambassador with the sole agenda of promoting the kingdom of God and glorifying the name of the Lord.

CHAPTER 1

THE MINISTRY OF LIGHT

You are the light of the world. A city on a hill cannot be hidden. **Matthew 5:14**

These are the words of Jesus to His disciples. He boldly declares that His disciples are the light of the world. If we, the believers in Christ Jesus, embody the world's light, it simply suggests that darkness envelops the world. Darkness must be present for light to perform. So, Jesus emphatically reveals to us one of the ministries of the saints. He didn't say we are the light of the earth but of the world. This implies that the earth already possesses its natural light—the daylight, sun, and moon. In the earth is a system called the world, which operates in and sponsors darkness. This system is ungodly and is not governed by the kingdom of God.

The system in the earth

The world is a system within the earth, and its ruler is Satan, the devil. Because the system belongs to the devil, when God looks upon the earth and sees this system, He perceives it as darkness. He does not see darkness merely as the blackness of the night, but rather as falsities or falsehood, evil, sin, immorality, disobedience, and all that He despises.

> *If you were of the world, the world would love its own:* ***but because you are not of the world****, but I have chosen you out of the world, therefore the world hates you.* **John 15:19**

If God has entrusted us as Christians with the ministry of light, then we bear a great responsibility to fulfill what He has called us to be and to do. Thus, we cannot live our lives just as we choose, because much depends on the ministry of light bestowed upon the believer by God.

Failure to live up to God's expectations in this ministry would only lead to more trouble and calamities on the earth. When we refuse to shine as light, we contribute to more problems for our nations, cities, and even families.

Now is the time for the believer in Jesus Christ to take up the mantle of the ministry of light and begin to shine, repelling all darkness and evil.

What is darkness

Darkness in both the Old and New Testament represents everything that is anti-God. It encompasses moral corruptness, wickedness, sin, and falsities. In Scripture, as light symbolizes truth, darkness is portrayed as the absence of truth.

To comprehend light and truly value the ministry of light, we must gain insight into what darkness is and understand what God deems as darkness.

For the ungodly, what God considers darkness may appear as light because they exist in the world and are under the influence of its ruler, Satan. It requires the revelation of light for someone to realize they have been in darkness all along. Light exposes darkness and drives it away.

> *The way of the wicked is like deep darkness; they do not know over what they stumble.* **Proverbs 4:19**

Everyone in the earth who is not born again is in darkness and under its direct influence. They may conclude or even assume that they are in the light, but darkness governs them.

Chosen out of darkness

In His great mercy, God reached out to mankind, offering His light to us. We were all in darkness, but His light shone in our hearts through Jesus Christ—the Light of the world. He then selected us to represent Him as light.

> *You are a chosen generation, a royal priesthood, an holy nation, a peculiar people; that you should show*

forth the praises of Him who has called you out of darkness into His marvelous light. **1 Peter 2:9**

God called us out of darkness. He took the initiative while we were immersed in and enjoying that darkness. We were headed for destruction, but He chose to guide us. Consequently, we are tasked with fulfilling the purpose for which He called us out of darkness: "to show forth His praises." This entails demonstrating His love and goodness in this wicked and dying world, embodying His character within us, so that our good works may be evident, leading the world to give glory to our heavenly Father

Let your light so shine before men that they may see your good works and glorify your Father which is in Heaven. **Matthew 5:16**

The believer has been chosen by the Lord to shine forth His light in the earth, revealing the difference between light and darkness. We are called to use the light of God within us to wage war against all that opposes the truth of the Word of God and to establish the ministry of light wherever we find ourselves.

And this is the verdict: The Light has come into the world, but men loved darkness more than light, because their deeds were evil. **John 3:19**

Jesus Christ, the Greatest Light

And the city has no need of sun or moon, for the glory of God illuminates the city, and the Lamb is its light.
Revelation 21:23(NLT)

In the New Jerusalem, the city of God, there will be no need for the sun and the moon as we have them today. The glory of God will illuminate the city, and the Lamb is its light. Essentially, Jesus Christ is both the glory and the Light that will illuminate and radiate the city. Can you imagine a city without the natural light and electricity as we know and use today? Such a city would be dark, a place where no life thrives, and depression reigns. However, this will not be the case for the New Jerusalem after God has judged all things.

The city will have no need for solar or lunar energy, electric or wind energy, as it will be powered by the "Light Himself," Jesus Christ—the Greatest Light. In Him, there is no darkness (1 John 1:15), and no shadow of turning (James 1:17); He is the perfect Light. All natural light has the ability to cast a shadow, including the sun and the moon.

In physics, a shadow is a dark area where light from a light source is blocked by an opaque object. Since Christ is Light Himself, anyone upon whom His light shines will experience no dark areas because His Light penetrates all angles or areas of that individual's life. If you are experiencing dark areas in your life, it simply means you have walked some distance away from the Light. Come closer, and He will illuminate every part of your life.

> *The people who walked in darkness have a great light; those who dwell in a land of deep darkness, on them has light shined.* **Isaiah 9:2 (ESV)**

Adam's sin and disobedience left mankind in deep darkness. From then on, humanity wallowed in darkness and appeared to relish every bit of it, heading straight towards God's wrath. In His divine providence, God had mercy on the predicaments of the human race and sent the Greatest Light, Jesus Christ, to illuminate the hearts of men and women willing to accept Him.

Now, as many have embraced Him, they have been infused with this Great Light. The believer has no option but to shine forth their light, as darkness bows and has no choice but to obey when light appears. The saints of God must daily be conscious of who they are and the ministry they are called into—the ministry of light.

The Lord Jesus Christ is that Greatest Light that has shone and continues to shine in the hearts of people all over the world. Because He is the Greatest Light, the very embodiment of light, we reflect His Light in our lives to the perishing world.

When Jesus spoke to the people, he said, "I am the light of the world. Whoever follows me will never walk in darkness, but will have the light of life."
John 8:12 (NIV)

What a profound declaration! I imagine some of His listeners might have pondered over this statement. What does He mean? How can He be the light of the world when we have the sun and the moon?

Jesus was essentially revealing the spiritual condition of the world—that it is engulfed in profound darkness, and He is the sole Light capable of illuminating it. Those who follow Him will not walk in darkness but will possess the light of life. The light we carry is the light of life. Everyone who is spiritually dead comes alive when they encounter this Great Light.

The light bearers

We are now the bearers of light. The Lord has fulfilled His ministry of light in the world. He came to introduce the true light, and having given us His light, He has passed on the baton to us. As Jesus Christ is not physically present on earth, the responsibility to bear His light now rests on our shoulders.

This is why He referred to believers as the light of the world (in Matthew 5:14). He understood that the ministry of light is the church's responsibility, and in doing so, He has provided everything necessary for us to carry His light.

"While I am in the world, I am the light of the world." **John 9:5**

Jesus declared that as long as He was in the world, He was the light of the world. He foresaw His ascension into heaven, recognizing that He would no longer physically dwell among men. However, through believers and His church, His light would continue to shine.

This significant ministry should be taken seriously by all believers. While some may engage in disputes over titles and positions within their local church assemblies, it's crucial to remember that the ministry of light extends beyond the church walls and into the world.

We are called to carry this light into our individual spheres and become the light there—God's light at our jobs, schools, communities, and in every aspect of our engagements. You, as a believer, are often the first representation of Jesus (light) that the ungodly encounter. Before you have the opportunity to introduce them to Jesus Christ, the Greatest Light, your life must already radiate Jesus to them. The era of hypocrisy is a thing of the past. The people in the world are hungry and searching for the true light. Many are genuinely seeking the Great Light in the wrong places. If only the saints of God would rise to their responsibility and fulfill the call of being the light of the world, our impact would be tremendous, leading people to walk in the true light and depopulating Hell.

Take full responsibility for the ministry of light—the world needs us. While the devil harvests souls into eternal darkness (Hell), the saints of God must not sit idly by, bickering over the unnecessary. This is a call for the body of Christ to "Arise and shine."

> *Arise, Shine; for your light has come! And the glory of the Lord is risen upon you. For behold, the darkness shall cover the earth and deep darkness the people; but the Lord will arise over you and His glory will be seen upon you.* **Isaiah 60:1-2**

The escalation of wickedness with each passing day is staggering. Unthinkable events are unfolding right before our eyes. Governments of nations seem clueless about the ongoing situation, as they are under the rulership of Satan and his worldly system. The ones with the answers happen to be the light bearers of God.

We must do something!

The era of sitting by and watching the house catch fire is over. God is calling on every saint, everyone who is born again, to arise and shine. The light is not about to come; it is already here. We are the carriers of the light, and we must not only speak about Christ Jesus, the Greatest Light, but we must also begin to live a life that truly radiates His person and all He stands for.

God is a Judge. This aspect of His nature will automatically judge darkness and evil. Where there is no one present as the light, the judgment of God is inevitable. When God was about to destroy Sodom and Gomorrah in the Old Testament, as recorded in Genesis 18, we observe this beautiful conversation between God and Abraham.

> *And Abraham came near and said, "Would You also destroy the righteous with the wicked? Suppose there were fifty righteous within the city; Would You also destroy the place and spare it for the fifty righteous that were in it? Far be it from You to do such a thing as this, to slay the righteous with the wicked, so that the righteous should be as the wicked; far be it from You! Shall not the Judge of all the earth do right?" So the Lord said, "If I find in Sodom fifty righteous within the city, then I will spare all the place for their sakes."* **Genesis 18:23-26**

Sodom and Gomorrah were destroyed not only because of their abominations but also because there weren't enough righteous people (light) within the cities. The role of the righteous in a country, city, or family goes beyond mere residence; it involves actively engaging in the ministry of light through prayers and intercession. This engagement makes the difference between God's wrath and judgment and God's mercy.

Every light bearer must recognize that they are the difference-makers, counted on by God to impact their world with the light of Christ within them. Lot, Abraham's nephew, failed to multiply the light he was supposed to be, and consequently, he witnessed the wrath of God in a place he once called home.

Upon being born again, we become the light that God sees in our family, community, cities, and nation. It is through us that His wrath is averted. Jesus Christ is the reason why a remnant will be saved—the Greatest Light that makes the difference between eternal life and eternal condemnation.

Could it be that high crime rates, drug abuse, divorce, and wickedness in cities and nations persist because the righteous are doing nothing or are ignorant of the ministry of light they are supposed to carry out? Perhaps depression and sickness ravaging through family lineages persist because the light bearers in those lineages have refused to take action.

Saints of God, it's time! Time to take our place, time to arise and shine, time to expel every darkness from our world through the power in the name of Jesus and the light He has bestowed upon us.

Often, we question God about why things are going wrong, and God gently responds that it is because we have decided to do nothing. Christ has given us the power to represent Him, and when things go wrong, He is not to be blamed. We must be responsible as managers He left with His light. What have you done with the light of God in you? Does your world feel your impact? I'm not referring to your weekly church activities but to how your life reflects Christ. Would your family, city, or nation be spared from judgment because of your ministry of light?

I firmly believe that God would have spared Sodom and Gomorrah if Abraham had resided there. No Scriptures record God speaking to or having a covenant with Lot. Abraham, on the other hand, bore the light, had a covenant with God, became a friend of God, and maintained a strong relationship with Him. If Abraham had been a citizen of Sodom and Gomorrah, his light could have spared those cities from judgment.

Making a difference as light in the world is not necessarily about numbers but about the quality of an individual's obedience, relationship, and walk with God. One person who has found God's grace and has a profound relationship with Him can have more impact in the world than a dozen uncommitted believers who wear the Christian badge for the sake of it.

Blame the righteous

The righteous should serve as the thermometer that controls the spiritual climate and temperature wherever they reside. The destruction of Sodom and Gomorrah wasn't solely due to their wickedness but also because there were not enough righteous people in those cities. This implies that the more the righteous shine their light, the more calamities and dangers they avert. When the righteous take full responsibility for their cities, both spiritual and natural disasters can be halted. Therefore, the saints must assume responsibility for the troubles besieging their cities because they have refused to shine their light.

As a righteous man and a prophet of God, Elijah exerted control over what transpired in Israel during his time. Despite the king's success in turning the hearts of the children of Israel away from God, Elijah, as a light, stood and declared what must be in the land, and heaven backed him up. If Elijah had refused to take action, the judgment of God on the land would have been more severe than the three-and-a-half-year famine (Reference: 1 Kings chapters 17 and 18). The writer of the book of James comprehended the role of Prophet Elijah well.

Elijah was a human being with a nature such as we have [with feelings, affections, and a constitution like ours]; and he prayed earnestly for it not to rain, and no rain fell on the earth for three years and six months. And [then] he prayed again and the heavens supplied rain and the land produced its crops [as usual]. **James 5:17-18 (AMP)**

The prophet Elijah, through the power of intense and earnest prayers, achieved what the ungodly Ahab couldn't. Elijah recognized that he had power over the land because he was the righteous man sent to lead the nation. Despite the unfavorable spiritual climate and the unwillingness of the king and his wife, Jezebel, to heed anyone, Elijah knew that stopping the rain would lead to famine, affecting everyone, including the king. If Elijah could accomplish such a feat, why are believers sitting by and watching things go wrong? Elijah served as the light in his nation, shining brightly. We have received the ministry and the power to do the same.

*I tell you the truth, **whatever** you forbid on earth will be forbidden in heaven, and **whatever** you permit on earth will be permitted in heaven.* **Matthew 18:18 (NLT)**

Imagine the immense power bestowed upon believers in Christ Jesus. The term 'whatever' encompasses everything— both good and bad—in your family, job, school, city, nation, and beyond. What you forbid, heaven forbids, and what you permit, heaven also permits. If you forbid untimely death in your family lineage, heaven forbids it. If you permit success in your life, heaven permits it. Whatever the righteous permit is backed up by heaven, and likewise, whatever they forbid, heaven forbids.

Secular governments worldwide have implemented laws that impact society, often because the righteous have failed to shine their light through prayer and intercession. Many of God's people tend to discuss and gossip about these matters rather than praying about them. When the laws are in place, complaints and frustration ensue, with some blaming God for not answering their delayed prayers.

In numerous Western countries, laws permitting same-sex marriages have been enacted. The topic of homosexuality and related laws is sensitive, and many preachers and righteous individuals, who are meant to be the light, choose to be politically correct or consider such behaviour as normal. Now, imagine if prophets like Elijah and the fearless prophets of God from the Bible were among us today—would they sit back and allow these sinful abominations to become law?

Foolish people are often given high positions, and the rich are left to fill lower positions. **Ecclesiastes 10:6 (GWT)**

In the eyes of God, the ungodly are considered foolish, while the rich are often deemed godly. In the world, you observe that those in authority are frequently the foolish ones, while the wealthy individuals sit back and watch events unfold. It is imperative for the godly to arise and take their positions. We must take our roles in politics, the media, the financial sector, medical arenas, the judiciary, the food sector, entertainment, the music world, and every other position we hold in our society today. The time for complaints and inaction is over. We are the light of the world, and we must shine, or darkness will continue to prevail.

Our society needs us. They need the light that God has deposited within us. We possess the transformative power they are searching for—our Christ and His righteousness.

When it goes well with the righteous, the city rejoices. And when the wicked perish there is joyful shouting. **Proverbs 11:10**

He prevents the godless from ruling so they cannot be a snare to the people. **Job 34:29**

God, on His part, favors the righteous to bear rule or be in positions of authority because the ungodly tend to ensnare the people and lead them into sin against God's principles. God blesses a nation when it is governed by the righteous, as the ungodly, lacking knowledge of the Lord, may make decisions that contradict God's will and standards, inviting judgment—especially when the righteous in that nation remain idle.

> *When the righteous increase, the people rejoice, but when the wicked rule, the people groan.* **Proverbs 29:2 (ESV)**

The greater the influence of the righteous, the more the people rejoice, and their well-being flourishes. Their lives are in harmony with God, and the land prospers. However, when the righteous permit the ungodly to take control, the people groan and suffer.

CHAPTER 2

LESSONS FROM THE
LAWS OF LIGHT

Natural light follows specific rules, generally simple yet capable of creating situations that may seem counterintuitive or perplexing. Within these natural rules of light, believers can extract valuable lessons to better understand their role as light-bearers and shine even brighter.

In the realm of natural light, there are three rules according to science:

A. Light travels in a straight line.

B. The farther you are from a light source, the dimmer the light.

C. The angle that a light beam makes when it hits a mirror (the angle of incidence) is the same size as the angle the beam makes when it bounces off the mirror (the angle of refraction).

Rule A: Light travels in a straight line

Lesson 1:
Commitment and Submission

Every believer represents our Lord and Savior Jesus Christ, the Greatest Light. If our light comes from Him, then we must be committed to continually follow Him for the light to remain effective. Deviating from following Jesus Christ leads to the loss and ineffectiveness of one's light. Christ is the source of our light, and the willingness to follow Him is termed submission and followership.

Being born again and becoming the light of the world is not enough. One must daily follow and submit to Christ to continue shining brightly. Our radiance depends on Him, and the more sincerely we follow the Lord wholeheartedly, the more we reflect His glory. Similar to how the moon recharges itself from the sun to produce light at night, the believer reflects what they receive from their Master, Jesus Christ—the Greatest Light.

There should be no interference between the Greatest Light (in Heaven) and the light of the world (the saints). The straight line connecting them must remain unbroken and unhindered at all times.

> *Then Jesus said to His disciples, "If anyone desires to come after Me, let him deny himself, and take up his cross, and follow Me."* **Matthew 16:24**

*Then Jesus spoke to them again, saying, "I am the light of the world. He who **follows** Me shall not walk in darkness, but have the light of life."* **John 8:12**

Notice in the verse that He didn't say, "he who follow Me," but "he who follows Me." The guarantee of sustaining the light you bear as a saint is your conscious and daily followership of Jesus. Anything short of this will leave the individual walking in partial light, and partial light is ineffective light. Therefore, it is possible for someone who once believed in Jesus to walk and wallow in darkness. Are you still shining? Do you daily radiate the light of God that you are to your world? Is your world feeling the impact of your light?

If Jesus is the source of your light, then you must follow Him in spirit and in truth (a straight line). You must not turn right or left. He alone "must become your reality and focus." Your decision to follow Him in a straight line determines how strong the light you carry will be and how effectively it will continue to shine.

*These are the ones who were not defiled with women, for they are virgins. **These are the ones who follow the Lamb wherever He goes**. These were redeemed from among men, being first fruits to God and to the Lamb.* **Revelation 14:4**

26

Rule B: The farther you are from a light source, the dimmer the light

Lesson 2
Communion/Fellowship

After the salvation of our souls, there is nothing that God desires more from us than communion with Him. The more we commune with Him, the more His glorious light shines through us. As His glory comes upon us, our light shines more brightly and becomes stronger.

When Jesus gave up his Ghost on the cross, the Bible declared that there was an earthquake and darkness in the very same hour (Matthew 27:45). The reason for this event is that when light goes out, even for a brief moment, darkness will invade that space. Since Jesus is the Light of the world, when He died on the cross and journeyed to Hades to free the souls of the righteous, darkness invaded the earth because the Light was temporarily absent from the earthly realm. The farther the earth was from Jesus when He died, the dimmer His light on earth, and darkness showed up. That's why I believe when He ascended into heaven, He did not leave the earth in darkness; He made us the light that shines in every darkness. Through our lives, His Light is visible to all men.

Draw near to God, and He will draw near to you. Cleanse your hands, you sinners, and purify your hearts, you double-minded. **James 4:8**

Some follow the Lord, yet they remain distant. Just following someone or a leader doesn't guarantee fellowship. Drawing near implies true fellowship—an interest in who they are and what they represent. To ensure our light continues to shine even brighter, we must draw near to God and not drift away. We must engage in communion with Him, fostering intimacy.

Intimacy with the Lord is crucial to ensuring our light radiates with the full strength intended by Him, as He is the source of everything we are

For in Him we live, and move and have our being; as certain also of your poets have said. For we are also his offspring. **Acts 17:28**

Staying connected to the Source of your light will generate more light to guide people in the right direction. We use light bulbs in our homes and offices, but no matter how powerful a bulb is, it is useless until connected to the light socket, through which the electricity current flows. The capacity of the light bulb determines the strength of light it produces. It is noteworthy that the electricity current is always on and flowing, day and night, constant and unchanged. However, light bulbs are replaced once in a while when their capacity and lifespan are spent.

This example illustrates that the Lord, our Light, is always constant, unchanged, consistently radiating power, grace, and mercy. When we lose touch with Him, we tend to lose our identity and strength. In Him (Christ Jesus), we live, move, and have our being. Apart from Him, we only produce darkness.

King David comprehended the significance of fellowshipping with the Lord, making it his life's goal to seek after God. In all his successes and failures, he stayed close to God.

> But as for me, the nearness of God is my good; I have made the Lord GOD my refuge, that I may tell of all Your works. **Psalm 73:28 (NASB)**

Drawing near to God is for our own good; we actually don't make Him bigger or better, but rather, He makes us bigger, better, and brighter. The farther you are away from your source of Light, the dimmer your light.

Jesus was inseparable from God the Father and God the Holy Spirit. He understood that for Him to achieve salvation for mankind, His relationship with the Father and the Holy Spirit must be the highest priority. He boldly declared to His followers that the source of His strength as Light is the

Father. He does what He sees the Father do, and He is in the Father, and the Father is in Him—always inseparable.

When He hung on the cross as sin for us, the Father (His Source) turned His face away from Him for a brief moment, and darkness fell everywhere. Because as sin on that cross, He was disconnected from His source.

> *Jesus gave them this answer: "Very truly I tell you, the Son can do nothing by himself; he can do only what he sees his Father doing, because whatever the Father does the Son also does.* **John 5:19 (NIV)**

Jesus couldn't be any clearer to His followers; He is the reflection of the Father, shining the same Light as the Father. That means He couldn't do it on His own; He needed the Father and the Holy Spirit to be the Light of the world. If He stayed connected to His Source, we must also be connected to Him at all times because He is our only Source.

Drawing near to the Lord can be measured by how hungry and thirsty one is for Him. Not for what He can give us or do through us, but for who He really is to us. The more we hunger and thirst after Him, the brighter He makes our light. The more we long for Him, the more we realize that no darkness can cling to our light. The presence of God is highly and extremely contagious; you cannot spend time with God and remain the same.

The level of your hunger and thirst for Him determines the capacity and strength of the light He stores in you.

I have come across believers who have been born again for almost 30 years, and the light they bear does not really reflect the God they gave their hearts to. I also know people whose light is felt tremendously, and they are just 3 to 5 years old in the Lord. The difference between these two is hunger and thirst for the Lord. The one is now familiar with the Lord and does not consider spending time with the Lord as important. While the other seeks the Lord with their life and cannot seem to get enough of Him, daily.

Rule C: The angle that a light beam makes when it hits a mirror surface (the angle of incidence) is the same size as the angle the beam makes when it bounces off the mirror surface (the angle of refraction)

Lesson 3
Impact

The impact felt when light is on can only continue when it stays connected, and it cannot be connected unless it follows a straight line. The capacity of the impact produced gives one a clue about how connected the light is. You cannot make so much impact as light in the world when your life has not been impacted by the Lord. This impact from the

Lord can only be achieved when you stay in fellowship with Him.

> *Heal the sick, raise the dead, cleanse those who have leprosy, drive out demons. Freely you have received; freely give.* **Matthew 10:8**

The ministry of light that believers in Jesus Christ are called into is to be felt in a world of sick, dead, and dying people—people who are contagious with leprosy, and those who are demon-possessed. The light you have received should be given freely. Don't keep the light for yourself because the light Christians bear is not for them; it is for the world, for the ungodly. We are called to extend God's light in a world of deep darkness, not just within the church. The gathering of many lights might only produce more light, and the effect may not be noticeable. However, the impact or ministry of a single light in a dying world would be greatly felt.

Give your light freely because you have received it freely. It is an error to commercialize the light God has entrusted in your hands. It is disheartening to see how many anointed and gifted individuals have turned the light (anointing, gifts, and talents) into a business, and they still wonder why their impact is minimal. God is not a businessman; He is not into buying and selling. Rather, His heart beats for impact—the impact your light has on others who are still in darkness and ignorance.

Do you know that you don't necessarily need a 'special anointing' to heal the sick, cleanse the lepers, and drive out demons? Although some people are specifically called by the Lord with an anointing in this regard, this anointing always comes with a mandate. But as a believer called out of darkness into the marvelous light of Christ, the light you carry is enough to do these things in the name of Jesus Christ.

Give what you are

You can only give what you are and have. The quality and quantity of what you carry or bear determine what you are able to give. The levels of your impact depend on your capacity. It is impossible to impact beyond your capacity. Your impact as light in this world can only be proportional to what you have received.

Jesus could make us lights because He is Light. The impact He made and is still making is a direct result of Him doing what He sees the Father do and giving what He has received from His Father.

> *So Jesus added, When you have lifted up the Son of Man [on the cross], you will realize [know, understand] that I am He [for Whom you look] and that I can do nothing of Myself (of My own accord or on My own authority), but I say [exactly] what My Father has taught Me.* **John 8:28 (AMP)**

This is because I have never spoken on My own authority or of My own accord or as self-appointed, but the Father Who sent Me has Himself given Me orders (concerning) what to say and what to tell. **John 12:49 (AMP)**

As Christians, if we claim to represent the Lord Jesus Christ in this world, everything around us **must** feel the impact of the light we bear and represent. To be satisfied with the status quo in this world as children of light is an insult to the kingdom of Light we are born into.

Expand Your Capacity

You can only give as much as you have. It is only the Lord who has the power to change our capacity spiritually. But we have our role to play for our capacities to be increased by the Lord. If the strength of the light bulb in your home is 60 watts and you desire more light, change the number of watts to a higher one. The capacity of light you bear as a child of God can be greatly increased; it takes some effort on your part for this to be realized. Since the life of God in us is from one level of glory to the next, no child of God should remain the same way as when he got born again. After a period of time, his life must be brighter and more colorful.

And we all, with unveiled face, beholding the glory of the Lord, are transformed into the same image from one degree of glory to another. For this comes from the Lord who is the Spirit. **2 Corinthians 3:18 (ESV)**

34

The transformation into His image that comes from beholding His glory can only be from one degree to another. It only increases for the believer; it cannot diminish as long as the believer keeps on "beholding His glory." His glory rubs off on us, and our capacity to bear more light increases. It could take years, months, or days to realize this. The desire of the Father is that the world will see the full image of Christ in the believer, just as the world saw the full image of the Father in Christ. Therefore, we must not stop desiring to be like Christ, as long as our hunger and thirst for Him increase. By His Holy Spirit, He expands our capacity to bear more of His light.

How to Expand Your Capacity

There are more ways that we can expand our capacities, but let's focus on these three aspects:

1. **Strong Desire**

2. **Selflessness**

3. **Responsibility**

Strong Desire

The more you desire the Lord, the more He fills you with His grace to desire Him more; the more He fills you and increases your desire, the more your capacity expands and increases. The more your capacity increases, the more the intensity of the light you can shine to your world. The more of God you can distribute in a world where darkness is loved and appreciated more than light. God is a Spirit and cannot be measured; He is limitless. He must be the very heartbeat of what we desire to be. He fills the heaven and the earth; He is the definition of capacity (Jeremiah 23:24). Like a newborn baby desires the breast milk of his mother, so every believer must desire the Lord. The mother has the natural ability and capacity to produce and store the milk. As long as the newborn baby desires the milk, there is always an uninterrupted flow and supply. Often, it is the baby that stops feeding because his capacity to retain milk is full, not because the milk has run out.

> *Blessed are they who do hunger and thirst after righteousness: for they shall be filled.* **Matthew 5:6**

> *"In His days Judah will be saved, and Israel will dwell securely; And this is His name by which He will be called, The Lord our righteousness."* **Jeremiah 23:6**

> *And of him are you in Christ Jesus, who of God is made unto us wisdom, and righteousness, and sanctification, and redemption.* **1 Corinthians 1:30**

Christ is our righteousness, and the more we hunger and thirst after Him, the more our capacity is filled with His character and life. In turn, we dispense His nature to our sick and dying world.

Selflessness

In all things, Jesus stands as the ultimate example of selflessness. When He came into this world, "He made Himself nothing" and embraced the nature of a servant (Philippians 2:7). Jesus didn't come for Himself or for personal gain; He came to illuminate His light and guide us in the Way.

> *"Even the Son of Man did not come to be served, but to serve, and to give his life as a ransom for many"*
> **Mark 10:45**

From a human perspective, Jesus surrendered His will to fulfil God's purpose (Luke 22:42). Selflessness goes beyond putting others first; it involves prioritizing God and His agenda. Going against the grain of human nature, being selfless is more challenging than succumbing to selfishness. It's natural to focus on ourselves, and societal pressures often encourage us to think selfishly.

> *Not so with you. Instead, whoever wants to become great among you must be your servant.* **Matthew 20:26 (NIV)**

As the light of the world, our attitude should be one of selfless service to God and others, following the example set by Christ. To influence the darkness of the world with the light we bear, we must be ready to serve. God always increases those who selflessly serve with the gifts, talents, anointing, and light they bear.

Selflessness is the highest form of service in the kingdom of God. When you decide to make a difference in someone's life or pursue a cause that positively impacts lives without seeking selfish gains, you exhibit selflessness.

Responsibility

Christianity transcends religion; it's a relationship with God through His Son, Jesus Christ. This relationship entails a responsibility to lead others into the same relationship with God (James 1:27). True Christians live not for themselves but for God and others. The walk with Christ is a call to forsake all and give all. Christians are called to make a difference in the world as lights.

Just as a bridge connects two points (A and B), Jesus took up the responsibility of restoring humanity to God through His obedience and sacrifice. Moses, chosen by God, led over three million people out of darkness (Egypt's bondage) into light (Canaan land's freedom). David, though untrained as a soldier, took responsibility to fight for Israel when Goliath threatened their existence. After being born again, believers become the difference between God and humanity, responsible to reveal God to the world. They are the difference between good and bad, sin and righteousness, victory and defeat. Believers are placed in the world to take up the responsibility as light and be the difference.

Many believers may not see the need to fully embrace the responsibility of being the light of the world. However, until we all recognize and embrace this responsibility, effectively repelling darkness, we cannot fully function in the role we are called into.

> *"Whatever you do, work heartily, as for the Lord and not for men, knowing that from the Lord you will receive the inheritance as your reward. You are serving the Lord Christ."* **Colossians 3:23-24**

> *Each of you must take responsibility for doing the creative best you can with your own life. Be very sure now, you who have been trained to a selfsufficient maturity, that you enter into a generous common life with those who have trained you, sharing all the good things that you have and experience. Don't be misled: No one makes a fool of God. what a person plants, he will harvest. The person who plants selfishness, ignoring the needs of others- ignoring God! – harvests a crop of weeds. All he'll have to show for his life is weeds! But the one who plants in response to God, letting God's Spirit do the growth work in him, harvests a crop a real life, eternal life. So let's not allow ourselves to get fatigued doing*

good. At the right time we will harvest a good crop
if we don't give up, or quit **Galatians 6:5-9 (MSG)**

Responsibility can be undertaken through both spiritual and physical means. Spiritually, believers can engage in the ministry of prayer, fasting, and prophetic declarations. Living a pure and holy life before God in our world differentiates us as the light of the world, refraining from engaging in worldly activities. Physically, believers can take a stand for morality and speak up against evil, wickedness, and abomination in the world. Many saints have compromised by accepting what is wrong simply because it is not happening around them or in their church.

Phinehas

In Numbers 25:1-13 and Psalms 106:30-31, the Israelites, on their way to the promised land, settled in Acacia Grove (Shittim) and engaged in harlotry, sacrificing to the idols of Moab. Despite being God's covenanted people and the light of the world, they committed abominations. God's anger was swift, and a plague broke out. God instructed Moses to bring the plague to a halt.

While Moses was in the tabernacle speaking with the tribal leaders, a man from the children of Israel brought a Midianite woman before them. The man's actions were so abominable that Phinehas, a priest, took matters into his own hands.

Now when Phinehas the son of Eleazar, the son of Aaron the priest, saw it, he rose from among the congregation and took a javelin in his hand; and he went after the man of Israel into the tent and thrust both of them through, the man of Israel and the woman through her body. So the plague was stopped among the children of Israel. And those who died in the plague were twenty four thousand. Then the Lord spoke to Moses, saying: Phinehas the son of Eleazar, the son of Aaron the priest, has turned back My wrath from the children of Israel, because he was zealous with My zeal among them, so that I did not consume the children of Israel in My zeal. Therefore say, "Behold I give to him My covenant of peace; and it shall be to him and his descendants after him a covenant of an everlasting priesthood, because he was zealous for his God, and made atonement for the children of Israel." **Numbers 25:7-13**

In the modern era, any pastor, leader, or Christian who takes matters into their hands as Phinehas did might be considered a murderer and face legal consequences. While society views such actions as murder or cruelty, God sees it as zealousness. Phinehas took the responsibility to stop a plague that had already claimed twenty-four thousand lives. His decisive action prevented further casualties, and God was so pleased with him that He made an everlasting covenant.

41

In today's context, taking responsibility and standing for God as lights in the world may come with physical consequences, but it pleases the Lord. Christians cannot afford to idly watch evil and wickedness proliferate without taking decisive action.

> *Therefore say, 'Behold I give to him My covenant of peace; and it shall be to him and his descendants after him a covenant of an everlasting priesthood, because he was zealous for his God, and made atonement for the children of Israel.'* **Numbers 25:12-13**

Phinehas did not act out of a desire for personal reward; his actions were driven by zealousness for God. While others wept in uncertainty, he took responsibility to alter the course of events in the land. God rewarded him, making an everlasting covenant that extended to his descendants. Zealousness involves a strong feeling of interest, passion, and enthusiasm, demonstrating eagerness and determination.

To be the light of the world, believers must embrace responsibility wholeheartedly, avoiding compromise and selfishness. God's call to ministry as lights requires a willingness to sacrifice everything. Waiting for the majority to act is futile; the responsibility to shine lies with each individual. God often works with those ready to take charge and be responsible.

Everyday Impact

Believers must understand that their lives should impact the world daily. Lukewarm attitudes are unacceptable, and the world should recognize believers by the daily contributions they make. Many Christians fail to realize the importance of impacting their world, keeping their light dim and almost useless. Just as Jesus made daily impacts during His earthly ministry, believers are called to do the same without excuses.

Who is Responsible?

In a democratic system, governments are held responsible for societal issues. Similarly, God holds light bearers responsible for darkness in the world. Light bearers must be accountable for not shining in the midst of darkness. Both spiritually and physically, there is no evidence suggesting darkness is stronger than light. When light appears in a dark room, darkness vanishes instantly.

> *This is how love is made complete among us so that we will have confidence on the day of judgement. **In this world we are like Jesus**.* **1 John 4:17 (NIV)**

Embracing Our Role as Lights

In this world, believers are called to emulate Jesus by shining their lights just as He did. Darkness cannot overpower light, but believers must be willing to step into the darkness. Many

Christians, however, fear the world and its darkness, retreating to their churches. They forget that light is created to confront darkness and that light is more powerful than darkness. It's time for believers to venture out into the world and be the light.

Blame Disunity

A significant hindrance to illuminating the world as the body of Christ is the lack of unity. Denominational walls have divided believers, hindering the impact they could make collectively. Instead of presenting a unified front, believers have hidden their light behind denominational barriers, contributing to the world's growing darkness.

Unity is crucial, as God intended the church to be one body, not fragmented into denominations. Jesus accomplished His divine purpose on earth because the Godhead was unified in Him, operating with one will and purpose. The church, representing the light of the world, can make a profound impact when united. Every born-again child of God is part of the church, and collective unity will expedite the process of lighting up the world.

> *I pray for them, I do not pray for the world but for those whom You have given Me, for they are Yours. And all Mine are Yours, and Yours are Mine, and I am glorified in them. Now I am no longer in the*

world, but these are in the world, and I come to You.
Holy Father, keep through Your name those whom
You have given Me, that they may be one as We are.
John 17:9-11

What a prayer!

The Lord foresaw the disunity within His church and, in anticipation, prayed for our unity as one body. He prayed that believers would work together, transcending differences in color, background, and race. The Lord's desire is for His church to reflect the unity within the Godhead, functioning as an unbreakable and unbeatable force that shines brightly as one powerful light.

The world faces tremendous challenges due to the lack of unity among the light bearers (the Church). Confusion reigns as they observe believers talking down on each other and criticizing what they are called to protect. Despite this, believers wonder why they are not making a more significant impact on the world.

God Separated Light from Darkness

In the book of Genesis, after God stepped into the earthly realm from eternity past, He did something remarkable. This act holds prophetic significance for the body of Christ (the church), which would emerge thousands of years later. After creating light, God separated it from darkness. This separation implies that, initially, the two were mixed together until God intervened to make the distinction.

> *And God said, let there be light; and there was light. And God saw that the light was good (suitable, pleasant) and He approved it; and God separated the light from the darkness.* **Genesis 1:3-4 (AMP)**

Therefore, it is possible to be the light and still be mixed with darkness. Until there is separation, the light would not shine at its full strength. How can the church be known as the light if we still partake in the ways of the ungodly? How can the ungodly recognize us as the difference-makers if our desires, mindset, and speech are exactly like theirs? We must be completely separated, with no compromise, and therein lies our power of impact. It was in reference to what happened in Genesis 1:3-4 that the apostle Paul made mention while writing to the Corinthians.

> *For God Who said, Let light shine out of darkness, has shone in our hearts so as [to beam forth] the Light for the illumination of the knowledge of the majesty and glory of God [as it is manifest in the Person and is revealed] in the face of Jesus Christ (the Messiah).* **2 Corinthians 4:6 (AMP)**

The following example is not intended to criticize anyone but to explain a crucial point.

I once shared the gospel with a lady who happened to know a brother that attended the same local church with me several years ago. This brother was very involved in church activities, but his lifestyle outside the church walls did not testify well of our Christian faith. While I was sharing the good news with this lady, she asked me if I knew this brother from the church, mentioning that he had also preached the same message to her. Excited that the gospel had already been presented to her, I asked why she did not respond to the message. She replied, "He preaches to me, and afterwards, I see him mingling himself with many shady businesses with guys around my neighborhood." She further explained that if that's the gospel he preaches, she doesn't want anything to do with it.

It's disheartening to see that many who carry the light are still mixed up with darkness, hindering the light of Jesus from shining in a world that needs Him the most. We were once like the ungodly, and out of our darkness (sin, lusts, carnal mindset), God shined His marvelous light. We cannot afford to be the same thing we are already being separated from.

Do not be unequally yoked together with unbelievers.
For what fellowship has righteousness with lawlessness?
And what communion has light with darkness? And

what accord has Christ with Belial? Or what part has the believer with an unbeliever? And what agreement has the temple of God has with idols? For you are the temple of the living God. As He has said: I will dwell in them and walk among them. I will be their God, and they shall be My people. Therefore, come out from among them and be separate, says the Lord. do not touch what is unclean, and I will receive you. I will be a Father to you, and you shall be My sons and daughters, says the Lord Almighty. **2 Corinthians 6:14-18**

This Bible text does not prohibit us from working or doing business with the ungodly (the world), attending the same school with them, or having them as our neighbors. However, it emphasizes that we should be different, having been born again. As the temple of God, we are vessels through which His light shines. The distinction between darkness and light becomes evident only when they are not mingled. Therefore, we are called to live separated lives.

CHAPTER 3

THE ATTRIBUTES OF LIGHT

Our actions and words should radiate the light of God. Every aspect of our character should reflect the qualities of our Lord Jesus Chris

Righteousness

> *God made him who had no sin to be sin for us, so that in him we might become the righteousness of God.* **2 Corinthians 5:21**

> *For the sin of this one man, Adam, caused death to rule over many. But even greater is God's wonderful grace and his gift of righteousness, for all who receive it will live in triumph over sin and death through this one man, Jesus Christ.* **Romans 5:17 (NLT)**

Righteousness is a gift from God through the sacrifice of His Son Jesus Christ. It is the very nature of God in man. We cannot be more righteous, nor can we have more righteousness than the one received when we got saved. Righteousness produces right living that is pleasant and acceptable to God. It is not merely abstaining from certain sinful acts like adultery, murder, stealing, or lying; rather, it is the nature of God induced in our spirit that produces right living and acts. Therefore, an ungodly person cannot be righteous, even if that individual has not committed specific acts of sin (Romans 3:23).

Because we have been made the righteousness of God in Christ Jesus, and it is a free gift for all who believe in the sacrifice of Jesus on the cross, God looks at the world differently. The ones He has made righteous are in the world, though not of the world, possessing His very nature that shines brightly in the midst of darkness, setting them apart.

There is a part of God that mankind, especially this generation, has not seen yet—His wrath and judgment. Devils and demons have experienced a level of the wrath and judgment of God, causing them to tremble at the thought. As recorded in scriptures, the patriarchs and the children of Israel encountered this side of God, as well as the great and unexplainable manifestation of His glory and power, leading them to fear for their lives. The generation that lacks the fear of God is the one that has not yet encountered Him.

It is a dreadful thing to fall into the hands of the living God. **Hebrews 10:31 (NIV)**

The presence of the righteous serves as a temporary deterrent to the wrath and judgment of God in the world. I believe that certain calamities and events are averted through the prayers and intercessions of God's righteous saints. The chaos that is anticipated after the rapture of the church is due to the departure of those who maintain order and safety in the world. As the light of the world, their absence allows darkness to prevail and run rampant.

For the mystery of lawlessness is already at work; only He who now restrains will do so until He is taken out of the way. And then the lawless one will be revealed, whom the Lord will consume with the breath of His mouth and destroy with the brightness of His coming. **2 Thessalonians 2:7-8**

According to this text, the Holy Spirit, residing in all believers, serves as the restrainer of the antichrist or the lawless one and will be removed with them at the coming of Christ. As long as the church (the believers, light bearers) is present on earth, the Holy Spirit remains, and darkness is rendered powerless. The full revelation of the lawless one, backed by the devil, will occur after the saints of God are taken away. This emphasizes the powerful role of the church as the light of the world.

Love (Agape)

Love is the greatest force in the universe. Since our God is love, and we emanate from Him, we carry this force called love. No Christian should struggle when it comes to love; our lives should radiate the love of God to our world. In a world filled with hate, the devil exploits this negativity to destroy souls. Deliberately giving the love of God creates an atmosphere to shine the light of God and counteract the destructive consequences of hate.

The ungodly person cannot produce the God-kind of love, as their spirit is tainted by sin. After conversion, the love they express becomes pure because their spirit is renewed, and they become the righteousness of God in Christ Jesus. Therefore, the love they exhibit in the world will have a profoundly impactful effect.

> *A new commandment I give unto you, that you love one another, as I have loved you, that you also love one another.* **John 13:34**

We are commanded by our Master Jesus to love and walk in love because we have His love in us. Since you can only give what you possess, the love of God in you should naturally flow into your world. Surprisingly, many believers don't grasp what it means to walk in love. Astonishingly, people engage in ministry for the Lord without recognizing that love is truly paramount. It doesn't matter what you do for God; if it is not born out of love, it is deemed unacceptable and useless.

Transmit God's love to your world, irrespective of how you are treated or how the world makes you feel. The love signal you emit will eventually unveil God's love to them. We are transmitters of the love of God, and it doesn't matter where we are—the force of love within us is potent enough to transform even the most hateful and degrading atmosphere.

Before Jesus came into this world, it was a tit-for-tat, an eye-for-an-eye situation. Humanity had not truly experienced God's love in the way and manner they received it from Jesus. This is because Jesus Christ is the very embodiment of love, revealed in human flesh. And now, He has given us a new commandment, nullifying the old: love one another, not only those who love you but also your enemies.

You have heard the law that says, 'Love your neighbor' and hate your enemy. But I say, love your enemies! Pray for those who persecute you! In that way, you will be acting as true children of your Father in heaven. For he gives his sunlight to both the evil and the good, and he sends rain on the just and the unjust alike. If you love only those who love you, what reward is there for that? Even corrupt tax collectors do that much. If you are kind only to your

53

friends, how are you different from anyone else? Even the pagan do that. But you are to be perfect, even as your Father in heaven is perfect **Matthew 5:43-48 (NLT)**

Our love transmission must extend beyond the confines of those we are comfortable with and those we easily get along with. This involves how we speak, our body language, and the practical aspect of helping those in need within our society. Love is a light that illuminates every form of darkness and hate. The love of God in us has the potent power to break through walls of religion and tradition. The first gospel the ungodly hear us preach is the love of God we show to them.

Love is a deliberate choice, always determined to reach both the good and the bad, including those we may consider undeserving of love. Love always gives, never condemns, and does not seek out weaknesses but covers a multitude of sins according to Scriptures.

Though I speak with the tongues of men and of the angels, but have not love, I have become sounding brass or a clinging cymbal. And though I have the gift of prophecy, and understand all mysteries and all knowledge, and though I have all faith, so that I could remove mountains, but have not love, I am nothing. And though I bestow all my goods to feed the poor, and though I give my body to be burned, but have not love, it profits me nothing. Love suffers long and is kind; love does not envy; love does not parade itself, it is not puffed up; does not behave rudely, does not seek its own, is not provoked, thinks no evil; does not rejoice in iniquity, but rejoices in the truth; bears all things, believes all things, hopes all things, endures all things. Love never fails. But whether there are prophecies, they will fail; whether there are tongues, they will cease; whether there is knowledge, it will vanish away. **1 Corinthians 13:1-8.**

Lighten up the world with the love of God inside of you. Show this dark world that we are alive and that God has made a way through His love, so that none should perish but that all will come to repentance.

Compassion

Compassion is birthed out of love. You cannot love without compassion, and you cannot have compassion outside the confines of love. Compassion is a feeling of deep sympathy and awareness of the suffering of another, accompanied by a strong desire to relieve and alleviate it. Until we begin to walk in compassion for the world around us, we will make little or no impact. Giving up on the ungodly too quickly is not the way. Saying things like, "It is their business, if they desire a change they should search for it," and "Thank God I am born again, they will be the ones going to Hell if they refuse the gospel," is not a compassionate approach. The delay of the rapture is a solid proof that God has not given up on the ungodly yet. His love will reach many who are genuinely seeking after Him. Therefore, we must allow the ungodly to experience the love and compassion of our God through us.

A heart full of compassion doesn't think ill or conclude on the ungodly but is always ready to show and give the love and compassion of God to everyone they come in contact with. In the eyes and understanding of the ungodly, they may not see anything wrong with their lifestyle, as many believe they are living a good life. However, through the eyes of God, their state is poor and sorrowful. It is our duty to see them through the eyes of God and have compassion for them. Jesus saw our poor state even before the first man was made (Rev. 13:8) and had compassion on us.

Your ungodly friends, neighbors, family members, and colleagues may have worldly goods, riches, and possessions, but their spiritual state is a poor one. The voice of compassion speaks louder than any audible voice of preaching from any pulpit. It is stronger than any religious doctrine known to man and transcends time. Compassion was the center and foundation of the ministry of Jesus; everywhere He traveled, His heart was felt through His interaction with everyone He encountered. The imprints of

His compassion changed their lives. We must deliberately do the same.

> *When He saw the crowds, He had compassion on them because they were confused and helpless, like sheep without a shepherd.* **Matthew 9:36 (NLT)**

The above Bible verse shows us how helpless mankind is. Jesus saw beyond their external appearances. Some may argue that they are comfortable in their lives in every way, but through the eyes of compassion, Jesus saw a people confused and helpless. It was in this context that He turned and spoke the following verses so profoundly.

> *Then He said to His disciples, "The harvest truly is plentiful, but the laborers are few. Therefore pray the Lord of the harvest to send out laborers into His harvest."* **Matthew 9:37-38**

Are you born again? Have you confessed that Jesus Christ is Savior and Lord? If your answer is yes, then you have been sent as a laborer into this dark world to shine the light of compassion and to bring in the harvest of souls.

Only laborers with compassion can really bring in the harvest Jesus desires. If He did it with compassion, we must also allow compassion to flow through our hearts. My definition of compassion is "complete passion." Until we are totally and completely full of passion for saving and impacting lives, the harvest will only be minimal.

Purity

Purity is one of the most controversial and unspoken topic in the body of Christ. Some suggests that once saved you can go ahead and live the life. While others relate this topic in a way that the hearer is left condemned and confused. From the Biblical point of view it is very clear, how we should go about with purity. Purity is light. Purity empowers the believer to shine his light even brighter in this dark world. It is the separating line between God's territory and that of our enemy, Satan.

Purity is a conduct, a lifestyle of conscious and daily separation from the immoral vices in the old sinful nature we left behind. Purity is essential in our walk with God, and it gives the light bearer full confidence and assurance to stand against darkness. Fear has no place where purity thrives. Purity simply means don't do what the ungodly does, don't indulge yourselves in their sinful activities.

Now then, brothers, you learned from us how you ought to live and to please God, as in fact you are doing. We ask and encourage you in the Lord to do so even more. You know what instructions we gave you through the Lord Jesus. For it is God's will that you be sanctified: You must abstain from sexual immorality. Each of you must know how to control his own body in a holy and honorable manner, with passion and lust like the gentiles who do not know God. Furthermore, you must never take advantage of or exploit a brother in this regard, because the Lord avenges all these things, just as we already told you and warned you. For God did not call us to be impure, but to be holy. **1 Thessalonians 4:1-7 (ESV)**

We can't practice what they do, live the same way and manner they live, and still be the light of the world to them. The more we decide to be pure before God and man in our hearts and deeds, the brighter our light shines. Purity is directly connected to the light we bear, and the easiest way to have that light corrupted is by indulging in the ways of the ungodly.

To the pure, all things are pure, but to those who are defiled and unbelieving nothing is pure; but even their mind and conscience are defiled. They profess to know God, but in works they deny Him, being abominable, disobedient, and disqualified for every good work. **Titus 1:15-16**

We are the light of the world, the body of Christ, the most powerful force on planet earth. Let's ensure that the light we bear shines through beyond the walls of our communities of shared belief to our sphere of contact.

Don't quench your light. While we are the light of the world, various factors can hinder, prevent, contaminate, or even destroy the light we bear. Every child of God has the responsibility of securing and protecting the light that God has made them to be. One of the saddest attitudes of our times is the lack of responsibility. Being responsible has become a thing of the past, with believers living their lives without a sense of responsibility. There's a tendency to shift blame and manufacture excuses to cover irresponsibility. Irresponsible attitudes are applauded over responsibility in the name of modernity, a regrettable trend.

God expects each of us to be responsible and represent Him in the way He desires, not how we have decided to. The Scripture says, *"Let your light so shine before men that they may see your good works and glorify your Father who is in heaven."* This verse places the responsibility of shining the light on the light bearer, suggesting that light can become dim if not allowed to shine. Allowing our light to shine produces good works, and through these works, men give glory to our Father. By refusing to let our light shine, we rob God of the glory He deserves. Light is not made for light but for darkness. If we refuse to "so shine" our light in this dark and evil world, what use are we as light?

Several obstacles can affect how our light shines in this world:

1. *Unconfessed and Unrepented Sins*

One cannot harbor darkness and expect the light to shine brightly. According to the Scriptures, a believer is supposed to confess and repent from acts of sin. When this is left undone, the gradual process of corrupting the light inside the individual begins. Believers must realize that light has no business with darkness and that righteousness has no dealings with wickedness (2 Cor. 6:14). The light we bear is holy, and demons tremble in the presence of a child of God who bears the light and keeps themselves unspotted from the affairs of the world (darkness). In an era of tolerance where everything evil is accepted and endorsed, believers must be careful not to find themselves tolerating what God hates or giving approval to things that God frowns upon. To continue shining brightly, we must confess and repent from acts of sin in these end times.

> *Do not be unequally yoked with unbelievers [do not make mis mated alliances with them, or come under a different you with them, inconsistent with your faith]. For what partnership have right living and right standing with God have with iniquity and lawlessness? Or how can light have fellowship with darkness?* **2 Corinthians 6:14 (AMP)**

2. *Ignorance*

Ignorance is the absence or lack of the usage of knowledge. Many believers are still struggling to understand who they are, unaware that they are the bearers of light, essential for dispelling the darkness in the world. They often depend on others for knowledge, overlooking the primary source of knowledge—the word of God.

The word of God serves as the Truth that dispels ignorance, offering us revelation knowledge of our identity in Christ Jesus. Unfortunately, the rejection of knowledge by many in the body of Christ has led to a rise in ignorance. Numerous individuals within the body of Christ are no longer firmly grounded in the truth found in the word of God. They are easily swayed to reject God's standards. If a light doesn't know its function, it can be easily overpowered by darkness. Ignorance acts as a destroyer of light, a seemingly harmless but insidious virus that infiltrates the lives of many. Despite boasting of knowledge, their actions often reveal a significant distance from the truth.

> *My people are destroyed for the lack of knowledge. Because you have rejected knowledge, I also will reject you from being My priest. Since you have forgotten the law of your God, I will forget your children.* **Hosea 4:6 (NASB)**

The rejection of knowledge is a sure way to the destruction of light. God, through His Word, has provided His church with the blueprint of heaven, outlining how to enforce the Father's will on earth. However, not all knowledge is accurate or right. Some knowledge may seem genuine, but when examined through the guidance of the Holy Spirit and the Word of God, it may prove to be false. The Bible serves as a tool to expose lies and darkness in the world, but understanding the revelations in Scripture is key to expelling darkness in our spheres of influence. As light bearers, God has made knowledge available to us, and to make darkness bow, we must wholeheartedly embrace His Word.

3. *Isolation*

Isolation is the initial step in quenching the light within us. No one can fulfill their role alone; we need each other in the body of Christ to shine brightly and subdue the forces of darkness prevailing in the world. Unfortunately, there are many "isolated lights" in the body of Christ today. Some choose isolation out of pride, thinking they know more than others, while others isolate themselves due to unpleasant experiences in their interactions within the Church. Regardless of the reasons, we are called to reconcile, forgive each other, and refuse isolation, to make a strong and lasting impact in our world. While a single charcoal can burn well, it cannot produce enough heat to cook a meal. In essence, we shine brighter together as one than when divided.

So we, who are many, are one body in Christ, and individually members one of another **Romans 12:5 (NASB)**

The world is in dire need of the light of Christ, and people long to experience the joy we find in Christ Jesus. It's time for all believers in Christ Jesus to set aside doctrinal differences and recognize that unity is crucial for bringing in the harvest of souls in these end times. This is a call for unity, urging believers to transcend isolation, ministries, or churches. If winning souls for Christ is a top priority, then together, our lights will defeat the darkness, no matter how much Satan and his cohorts believe they can inflict damage on the church.

4. *Lukewarmness*

The Lord desires us to be alive, active, and burning with His light within us. He prefers us to be either hot or cold rather than lukewarm. Lukewarmness involves having or showing little zeal or enthusiasm, indicating indifference about one's choices, decisions, and stance. This lukewarm spirit has been present since the days of John the Revelator, and God sternly addresses it in His revelation to John.

Lukewarmness doesn't happen suddenly; it begins gradually in the heart of the believer, leading them into a state of spiritual complacency. Lukewarm believers have the form of

God in them but deny its power. They have gradually lost their initial love for God and the things concerning His kingdom. The light of God in them has lost its spark and is progressively dying out, and they seem indifferent to it.

Reaching our world and accomplishing mighty things for the Lord is impossible with a lukewarm spirit. Anything causing you to become indifferent about your love for God and His gospel is from the pit of hell, designed to quench your light completely.

> *So, because you are lukewarm-neither hot nor cold-I am about to spit you out of my mouth.* **Revelation 3:16 (NIV)**

To avert the inevitable judgment of God spitting us out of His mouth due to lukewarmness, a prompt decision is essential to become actively engaged in God and His gospel. The danger of being cast aside and replaced by another to fulfill God's plan and purpose should be avoided. It's crucial to awaken yourself or align with brethren whose fire is alive and active, allowing their fervor to reignite the flame you've lost.

> *Therefore, I remind you that you stir up the gift of God, which is in you by the laying on of my hands.* **2 Timothy 1:6**

Prayer/Declaration:

Heavenly Father, I express my gratitude in the name of Jesus Christ, my Lord and King, for transforming me into a radiant light. A light that no darkness can extinguish. I boldly declare that I am shining, radiating, and guiding many from the dominion of darkness into the kingdom of God. My light is vibrant, illuminating the love and essence of God to everyone within my sphere of influence. I thank You, Father, for every opportunity You have bestowed upon me to radiate Your light. I now declare that nations will be drawn to my light, and kings will be attracted to the brilliance of my dawn, in the glorious name of Jesus. Amen

CHAPTER 4

A CITY ON A HILL

You are the light of the world. A city on a hill cannot be hidden. **Matthew 5:14**

As believers, whether we acknowledge it or not, Jesus declared that we are like a city located on a hilltop that cannot be hidden. This means that once an individual becomes born again, they are exposed to both the natural and spiritual world. In the natural world, they serve as a beacon of light and a lighthouse to safety. In the spiritual realm, they become a potential threat to darkness, a powerful tool in God's hand.

It is the believer's ministry to be a city on a hill, an example and guiding structure directing people to God. Your life should be a visible testimony, helping the ungodly find their way to God. God, humans, angels, and demons are observing your life, and you cannot afford to live below the ministry you've been called to.

Just as lighthouses were crucial for mariners in the past, serving as a guiding light when approaching land, believers are called to be a guiding light for those seeking God. Jesus referred to His followers as a city on a hill, emphasizing the power of unity and collectiveness. Disunity is an enemy that hinders the shining of our light.

The unity and collective efforts of believers, like houses forming a city, enhance the visibility of Christ's light. When believers are united, the world can truly see Christ in them from afar. They appreciate the price He paid to make believers who they are.

The analogy of lighthouses also highlights the importance of Christians leading the way for the ungodly, helping them navigate away from dangers. Believers should be the ones guiding others out of hazards and towards safety.

Living like Christ and following His words is the key. If all Christians were to live exactly like Christ and adhere to His teachings, the impact would be profound, and there would be no need for excessive words to convey the gospel.

In essence, believers are called to be a powerful collective force, shining the light of Christ, leading others out of darkness, and serving as beacons of hope and guidance for those in need.

By the blessing of the influence of the upright and God's favor (because of them), the city is exalted, but it is overthrown by the mouth of the wicked.
Proverbs 11:11 (AMP*)*

May we indeed become the city on a hill that attracts people to God, and may our lives serve as a mirror reflecting the dangers and guiding them away from harm. It's essential to recognize that our character and lifestyle matter significantly to this dark world. If our lives don't align with the description of being a city on a hill as Christ spoke of, it's time for introspection.

Prayer/Declaration:

In the name of the Lord Jesus Christ, I declare today that I am a city on a hilltop. I am a sign that attracts men and women to the Lord. My life is a reflection of the grace of God to as many as I shall encounter from today. I shall no longer be hidden. Father, thank You for making me visible to my world. In Jesus mighty name, amen.

CHAPTER 5

THE SALT OF THE EARTH

*You are the salt of the earth; but if the salt loses its flavor, how shall it be seasoned? It is then good for nothing but to be thrown out and trampled underfoot by men. **Matthew 4:13***

Salt is life – a statement that holds true not only for natural food diets but also in the context of Matthew 4:13. It remains a prevalent ingredient in our diets, and we often underestimate its significance until doctors place us on a salt-free diet. Then, to our distress, we realize that many enjoyable and convenient things contain salt. Let's explore some benefits of edible salt to the human body before delving into the spiritual benefits of being the salt of the earth.

Benefits of Edible Salt:

1. Salt enhances the taste of food, adding a satiety factor that makes meals enjoyable. The right salt content encourages mindful eating, prioritizing quality over quantity.

2. Salt aids in blood sugar control by improving insulin sensitivity. A low salt diet increases insulin resistance, and even moderate dietary salt restriction can cause systemic insulin resistance.

3. A pinch of salt on the tongue may help improve allergic reactions or asthma attacks.

4. Salt contributes to better sleep quality, possessing anti-stress and anti-excitatory qualities through the suppression of stress hormones and an increase in metabolic rate.

5. The body needs salt to maintain proper stomach pH. Hydrochloric acid in the human stomach reacts with sodium chloride (salt), forming the foundation for good food digestion.

If natural healthy salt can offer these benefits to our human body, imagine the depth of understanding required for our role as the salt of the earth. The Lord was unequivocal when making this statement – He didn't suggest we could be like salt or should resemble it; He emphatically called us the salt of the earth. This means we have been given the responsibility of amplifying and preserving.

Salt in Ancient Times: Salt has played a crucial and integral role in the world's history, woven into the daily lives of countless civilizations. Even today, the history of salt

71

continues to touch our daily lives. The word 'salary' finds its origin in 'salt.' Salt was highly valued, and its production was legally restricted in ancient times, serving as a method of trade and currency. The word 'salad' originated from 'salt' among the Romans when they began salting greens and vegetables. It stands out as one of the most effective and widely used food preservatives, even used by Egyptians to preserve their mummies.

Salt's importance dates back to 6050 BC, playing a vital role in economics. Trade in ancient Greece involved exchanging salt for slaves, giving rise to the expression 'not worth his salt.' Early Roman soldiers received special salt rations known as 'salarium argentum,' coining the English word 'salary' from this practice.

Little wonder the Lord Jesus Christ has given believers the ministry of being the salt of the earth. We are called to add flavor to our world and bring preservation in every capacity. The amplified version provides a clearer translation of the same verse.

> *You are the salt of the earth, but if the salt has lost its taste (its strength and quality), how can its saltiness be restored? It is not good for anything any longer but to be thrown out and trodden underfoot by men.* **Matthew 4:13 (AMP)**

We need to grasp the understanding that God is Spirit, and He evaluates all things based on His standards. Only those who are alive in Him spiritually can connect with Him. The call to be the salt of the earth is not for everyone but for those who have accepted Christ as their Lord and Savior and have chosen to make a defining impact on the earth.

We add taste to the earth

Given that every offering from the sinful nature is an abomination to God, it is the children of God who bring taste to the earth. Our presence in the world adds flavor because only the born-again individuals and their offerings are acceptable to God.

> *Can something tasteless be eaten without salt, or is there any taste in the white of an egg?* **Job 6:6 (NASB).**

Can the world, so steeped in sin, be acceptable to a Holy God without His children who are the salt of the earth? When God looks upon the earth, it's His children who bring taste to an otherwise unpalatable world full of rot and decay. In the Old Testament, God gave the children of Israel a crucial commandment regarding salt. Since the Old Testament serves as a shadow of the real thing (Hebrews 10:1), the use of salt in the offerings of the Jews, among other things, was symbolic of the saints of God whom Jesus called to be the salt of the earth.

> *You shall season all your grain offerings with salt. You shall not let the salt of the covenant with your God be missing from your grain offering;* **with all your offerings you shall offer salt.** **Leviticus 2:13 (ESV)**

Christianity serves as the salt of the earth. Without you and me, the world would lack the flavor it needs before God. Therefore, the Lord expects us to live out the ministry of flavoring the earth with His love, mercy, and goodness. The Lord addressed the saints in Laodicea through John's revelation, and I believe it is highly relevant to us today, as we are called to bring taste and flavor to the earth.

> *These are the words of the Amen, the faithful and true witness, the ruler of God's creation. I know your deeds, that you are neither cold nor hot. I wish you were either one or the other! So, because you are lukewarm- neither hot nor cold- I am about to spit you out of My mouth.* **Revelation 3:14-16 (NIV)**

As long as we are in His mouth, we should represent who we are – tasteful and flavorful. He warns us that He will spit us out when we refuse to be hot or cold. When we fail to live according to His ways and define our Christianity based on

His Word, we risk the chance of being cast down on the street and trampled upon by men.

One of the challenges facing end-time believers is defining what they stand for. Many believers have become lukewarm – neither fully committed to being disciples of Christ nor wholly embracing ungodliness. They often thrive on the premise of being politically correct, blending with the world to produce a taste that God calls lukewarm. The inevitable consequence of this ungodly behavior is the risk of being "spit out."

As Christians, as believers in Jesus Christ, the Son of the living God, we are sent on a mission. We have been given the ministry of adding value and taste to our world, our sphere of contact. The human instinctive reaction is to quickly discard a beverage or any other product that has lost its usual taste. If humans discard a product that has lost its taste, can we expect the Almighty God to keep on tolerating our distasteful ways of not being who He has called us to be? Add taste to your world. Don't compromise the strength and quality of being the salt of the earth.

We Preserve the Earth

To preserve means to keep something as it is, especially to prevent it from decaying or protect it from being damaged or destroyed. It is also to keep alive or in existence; make lasting. Furthermore, it is to keep safe from harm and injury;

protect or spare. To maintain something in its original or existing state.

Natural salt is widely and historically known for its preservative properties. Salt is water absorbent and removes water from food. In the absence of water, bacteria cannot multiply. Bacteria are dangerous, and one of the major means through which they spread is water. When salt is added to that environment, it dries up the water by absorbing it, creating an atmosphere unsuitable for germs and bacteria to thrive.

Christianity preserves the earth. We are the ones keeping the gates of Hell from breaking loose. Because God the Holy Spirit is in the earth, indwelling the saints, the world is kept together. It's no wonder that all Hell will break open after the rapture of the church because the salt of the earth is no longer present. Since God cannot destroy the righteous with the wicked, as long as the righteous are in a place, that place is preserved because of them. The earth is preserved because of you, as you are born again and on the Lord's side, called to the ministry of preservation.

> *For the Lord loves justice, and forsakes not His saints; they are preserved forever: but the descendants of the wicked shall be cut off.* **Psalm 37:28.**

In our modern-day society, many may not fully comprehend the worth of salt. In ancient times, lacking refrigerators or freezers for food preservation, salt served as the sole means of preserving perishable items prone to quick decay due to heat.

> Therefore, when Jesus declared to His followers, *"You are the salt of the earth. But if the salt loses its taste, how can it be made salty again? It is no longer good for anything, except to be thrown out and trampled underfoot by men."* **Matthew 5:13**

Jesus was conveying that as individuals separated from the world, with a relationship with God the Father, they held significance for the world. However, if they lost the essence of their belief, their value diminished. God had a vision, and they were integral to that vision – to ensure their faith or belief reflected His heart to everyone they encountered.

God's heart and vision are explicitly stated for the world to witness. It is an open declaration that believers are called to announce to the world: *"For God so loved the world that He gave His only begotten Son, that whosoever believes in Him should not perish but have eternal life"*(John 3:16).' Now, that agape love (God's love) is sought through believers like you and me, and God's people everywhere. Someone out there is earnestly searching for His love, someone desires to be seasoned by the salt within you. Will you respond to this call? Always remember, regardless of how dreadful and chaotic our world may seem, God has chosen ones whom He has called to be salt. Hallelujah!

Salt a symbol of covenant

> *Should you not know that the Lord God of Israel gave the dominion over Israel to David forever, to him and his sons by a covenant of salt?* **2 Chronicles 13:5**

And this is God's covenant to king David;

> *My covenant will I not break, nor alter the word that have gone out of My lips. Once I have sworn by My holiness; I will not lie to David: His seed shall endure forever, and his throne as the sun before Me, it shall be established forever like the moon, even like the faithful witness in the sky.* **Psalm 89:34-37**

A covenant of salt is profoundly robust, representing an enduring and binding agreement, whether for a while or forever. This metaphor used by Jesus signifies the desire for us to exhibit qualities of endurance. He urges us to remain faithful despite circumstances, as His word is unfailingly sure. Much like salt, symbolizing endurance, His word endures for everlasting.

Given that salt is a symbol of covenant, and we are deemed the salt of the earth, God's people on earth represent His enduring covenant of salvation to all. If one can be saved, then anyone can be saved. As those who have become the salt, it is our responsibility to spread the message of being the salt of the earth through the completed work of our Lord and Savior, Jesus Christ.

Salt purifies

Salt has purifying properties, as demonstrated in ancient times when newborns were rubbed with salt for cleansing.

> *On the day you were born, no one cared about you. Your umbilical cord was not cut, and you were never washed, rubbed with salt, and wrapped in cloth.*
> **Ezekiel 16:4**

A genuine disciple of the Lord Jesus is deemed pure in the eyes of God, thus contributing purity to the earth as long as the Lord tarries. In the divine plan, a child of God possesses purity regardless of their location. Their presence purifies the region, workplace, school, or neighborhood they find themselves in. Notably, Elisha's initial miracles involved the demonstration of salt.

> *One day the leaders of the town of Jericho visited Elisha. "We have a problem, my lord," they told him." This town is located in pleasant surroundings, as you can see. But the water is bad and the land is unproductive. Elisha said, "Bring me a new bowl with salt in it." So they brought it to him. Then he went out to the spring that supplied the town with*

water and threw salt into it. And he said, This is what the lord says: "I have purified this water. It will no longer cause death or infertility." And the water has remained pure ever since, just as Elisha said. **2 Kings 2:19-22**

Since Elisha held the prophetic mantle, he foretold events to the saints of the New Testament, showcasing the might of God by using salt to purify water and render the land fertile.

No matter the contamination of a source or the desolation of a place, introducing the salt of the earth (disciples of Jesus Christ) transforms the atmosphere, turning what is wrong into what is right.

It is an oversight for the salt of the earth not to influence their world with godliness and positive change. Being Christ-like involves more than idleness, especially when bestowed with power and authority. Your life must epitomize the qualities of salt and bear witness to the power of the kingdom to which you belong. Gone are the days when we remain silent as the ungodly tarnish our saltiness; we must distance ourselves, define our beliefs, take a firm stance, and impact them with our entirety. Every child of the living God is salt in the earth.

If anyone, then, knows the good they ought to do and doesn't do it, it is sin for them. **James 4:17 (NIV)**

Prayer/Declaration

Father, in the name of Jesus Christ, I acknowledge Your Word that declares me as the salt of the earth. Embracing this ministry, I commit to impacting lives with my saltiness, guided and assisted by the Holy Spirit. I pledge to walk in a manner worthy of Your calling on my life to be the salt of the earth. Henceforth, my testimony shall resonate with the words, "Oh, come taste and see that the Lord is good, amen."

CHAPTER 6

THE MINISTERS OF THE FRAGRANCE OF CHRIST

Our lives are a Christ-like fragrance rising up to God. but this fragrance is perceived differently by those who are being saved and by those who are perishing. **2 Corinthians 2:15 (NLT)**

I have yet to encounter any reasonable individual who relishes offensive odors or desires to be in a filthy and disgusting environment saturated with unpleasant air pollution. The sensible approach is to diffuse or spray a pleasant perfume or fragrance into the air to alleviate the atmosphere from foul corruption. Among many reasons, the prevention of bad and stinking odors is why we use fragrances.

The fragrance market is a multibillion-dollar industry. In 2020 alone, the global fragrance market was estimated to be worth approximately USD 43.3 billion and is projected to reach a revised size of $54.6 billion by 2027. Surprisingly, none of these perfume brands seems to appeal to our Holy God. As long as there are still foul smells on Earth and people desire to feel good about themselves and their individualities, humans will continue to spend billions on fragrances.

Reasons we use fragrance

According to the dictionary, perfume is defined as a substance, extract, or preparation designed to diffuse or impart an agreeable or attractive scent, particularly a fluid containing fragrant natural oils extracted from flowers, woods, and other sources. It is the scent, odor, or volatile particles emitted by substances that smell agreeable. Meanwhile, the word fragrance is the quality of being fragrant; a sweet or pleasing scent.

In our modern society, people wear perfumes for different reasons. Nevertheless, all perfumes or fragrances can only be noticed by one part of our body—the nose. People have been drawn to scented oils, perfumes, and other fragrances since ancient times. Nowadays, fragrances are also used in various relaxation procedures, such as aromatic baths, saunas, and steam rooms. Most people choose products based on how they smell, believing that specific aromas trigger specific hormones in the body with a particular impact. Some scents freshen you up, while others provide a more pleasant, happy, and romantic feel to the senses.

Among the many reasons fragrances are used, let's explore a few:

1. To keep foul odor away: Some individuals naturally perspire a lot or encounter unpleasant body odors due to their occupation. Wearing perfumes helps prevent hesitation when meeting others, increasing confidence and eliminating self-consciousness about body odor.

2. To show individuality: Fragrances are worn to express individuality. People choose perfumes based on mood, occasion, time, and more. The scents one wears can leave a lasting impression on others, serving as a means to create a memorable identity.

3. For therapeutic therapies: Since smell significantly impacts the body, many use fragrances for therapeutic purposes. Some scents induce calmness, peace, and a serene mental state, while others rejuvenate the mind and senses. Fragrances are considered a therapeutic tool to combat stress and bring liveliness to a dull and boring life.

The Biblical perspectives of fragrance

We are referred to as the fragrance of Christ because of Christ in us, the hope of glory. His life within us has made us a pleasing aroma, first to God and then to humans. Christ is the ultimate sin offering, a pleasant aroma to God, and now, He has transformed us into a fragrance of total sacrifice.

And walk in love, as Christ also hath loved us, and hath given Himself for us an offering and sacrifice to God for a sweet- smelling aroma. **Ephesians 5:2**

Perfume serves a significant role in Scriptures, notably in the preparation of a body for burial. In Matthew 26:6-13, there is an account of a woman who poured a highly valuable perfume on Jesus from an alabaster box, estimated to be worth an entire year's wages, as noted by Bible scholars (Luke 14:5). Despite the criticism and disapproval from others, Jesus not only praised the woman but also commended her actions.

But when Jesus was aware of it, He said to them, "Why do you trouble this woman? For she has done a good work for me. For you have the poor with you always, but Me you do not have always. For in pouring this fragrant oil on My body, she did it for My burial. Assuredly I say to you, wherever this gospel is preached in the whole world, what this woman has done will also be told as a memorial to her." **Matthew 26:10-13**

She chose to pour her expensive fragrance on Jesus rather than keeping it stored in the alabaster box for mere admiration. She comprehended the purpose of her costly oil.

Noah, a character from the Old Testament, received instructions from God to build an ark to rescue himself, his family, and various birds and animals. After the flood, Noah decided to present a sacrifice to God. He offered a burnt offering of clean animals and birds to God upon leaving the ark. Noah's sacrifice emitted a pleasing "aroma" to God. God found favor in Noah's sacrifice because it served as a satisfaction or propitiation of God's righteous requirement for atonement. God was pleased because the offering and gesture came directly from Noah without any specific instructions from God regarding the sacrifice, yet it met God's satisfaction.

> *And Noah built an altar to the Lord and took of every clean (four footed) animal and of every clean fowl or bird and offered burnt offerings on the altar. When the Lord smelled the pleasing odor (a scent of satisfaction to His heart), the Lord said to Himself, I will never again curse the ground because of man, for the imagination (the strong desire) of man's heart is evil and wicked from his youth; neither will I ever again smite and destroy every living thing, as I have done.* **Genesis 8:20-21**

Does God experience smells in the same way humans do?

Considering His throne isn't on Earth, does He perceive scents with His nostrils or His heart?

By delving into the Scriptures, we can gain insight into how God perceives aroma.

In the book of Leviticus, the phrase "an aroma pleasing to the Lord" is mentioned sixteen times. The fragrance of a sacrifice holds specific importance to God, not merely for its scent but for what that scent symbolizes – substitutionary atonement. The New Testament reveals Christ as the ultimate sacrifice for sin, the ultimate propitiation.

Ephesians 5:2 states, *"Christ loved us and gave himself up for us as a fragrant offering and sacrifice to God."* Christ is the only One capable of providing an eternally pleasing sacrifice. He is the One of whom the Father says,

> *You are My beloved Son, in whom I am well pleased.*
> **Mark 1:11**

Christ's Fragrance Dispensers

We serve as bearers of Christ's fragrance, embodying God's perfume in a world marked by unpleasant odors. Our impact is perceived uniquely by those who have embraced salvation and those yet to do so. Among the saved, we are recognized as a pleasing and delightful aroma, while to those who are perishing, our presence may be akin to an offensive odor.

For we are the sweet fragrance of Christ [which exhales] unto God, [discernible alike] among those who are being saved and among those who are perishing: To the latter it is an aroma [wafted] from death to death [a fatal odor, the smell of doom]; to the former it is an aroma from life to life [a vital fragrance, living and fresh]. And who is qualified (fit and sufficient) for these things? [who is able for such a ministry? We?]. **2 Corinthians 2:15-16 (AMP)**

Aroma of Christ: Embracing the Divine Scent

The fragrance we carry is perceived differently by those aligned with God and those who are ungodly.

To the perishing

Many Christians feel offended when met with disdain and hostility from the ungodly, especially in workplaces, schools, and neighborhoods, due to their allegiance to Christ. Some believers may question the validity of the message they represent, given their apparent unpopularity. We are the fragrance, and Christ is the Brand. Just as not everyone enjoys every brand of fragrance in the market, it should not surprise believers when the world rejects them, considering to the perishing, 'We are an offensive odor.' We may not smell pleasant to their spiritual nostrils because they are still under Satan's influence, diffusing a different aroma to them.

Consequently, some believers have blended with the world, mixing their fragrance with the world's scent. Others have entirely abandoned their unique fragrance, dispensing the devil's aroma of sin, pride, and disobedience. Do not be perturbed when the world rejects you; your Master was also rejected. We are called to dispense the fragrance of Christ, and through the Holy Spirit, the Distributor of the Brand, many among the ungodly will eventually be drawn by the scent of the gospel of Christ.

Top fragrance companies in the world would fiercely protect their products against imitation. Christ expects us to maintain His fragrance in our lives. He disapproves of anyone trying to fake, imitate, or blend with the world. We are called to stand out, so when the world encounters the fragrance we wear, they don't get confused. It breaks my heart when an ungodly person questions the genuineness or authenticity of the faith of a child of God because they are not dispensing the right aroma of Christ. We must flee anything that would corrupt the brand we represent and shun any appearance compromising the quality of what we carry.

Remember, "We are to God the fragrance of Christ among those who are being saved and among those who are perishing. To the one, we are the aroma of death leading to death…"

To those who are saved

For those who are saved, we are an aroma of life to life, a vital fragrance that is living and fresh. Together, our scent becomes stronger, overpowering every foul odor the enemy might diffuse among us. We are to lift and support one another, recognizing that we are of the same Brand (Christ) and the same Distributor (the Holy Ghost).

Unity enhances the acceptance of our Brand by those perishing. Only an unwise businessperson criticizes their products; instead, they promote and speak well of them to make a profit and stay relevant in the market. Why, then, do we tear each other down and expect the world to embrace the fragrance we promote?

One significant trait of fragrance is that it cannot be hidden. Once sprayed, anyone in that atmosphere will smell and recognize the scent. Do not hide who you are any longer; you are the fragrance of Christ, first to God and then to humans.

If God has accepted you as fragrant, who is man to belittle or reject you? Do not compromise your beliefs in a world where evil aromas are chosen and applauded as good. The scent of your fragrance may not be appreciated by everyone, and knowing this will give you the confidence to be who you are in God and to people.

Therefore, since we have this ministry, as we have received mercy, we not lose heart. But we have renounced the hidden things of shame, not walking in craftiness nor handling the word of God deceitfully, but by manifestations of the truth commending ourselves to every man's conscience in the sight of God. But even if our gospel is veiled, it is veiled to those who are perishing, whose minds the god of this age has blinded, who do not believe, lest the light of the gospel of the glory of Christ, who is the image of God, should shine on them. For we do not preach ourselves, but Christ Jesus the Lord, and ourselves your bondservants for Jesus' sake. For it is the God who commanded light to shine out of darkness, who has shone in our hearts to give light of the knowledge of the glory of God in the face of Jesus. **2 Corinthians 4:1-6**

Prayer/Declaration

My heart's desire, Lord, is to diffuse Your love into this dying world. I yearn to authentically represent You and Your word, regardless of the situations or circumstances I may find myself in. Through my life and conversations, may hearts and lives be turned towards You. Holy Spirit, be my guide, helping me dispense the fragrance of Christ everywhere I go. May no foul odor emanate from my life, but only the sweet scent of Christ — the aroma of grace, peace, and Your divine order. In Jesus' wonderful name, I pray. Amen.

CHAPTER 7

MINISTERS OF
RECONCILIATION

Every apostle, pastor, deacon, or ministry leader is, first and foremost, a believer in Jesus Christ. They are considered Christians before being called to a specific office of service within the body of Christ. Their primary calling is to win the lost at all costs, being the voice of one crying in the wilderness, pointing all individuals to the redemptive work of Christ on the cross

Why from now on know we no man after the flesh: yes, though we have known Christ after the flesh, yet from now on know we him no more. Therefore if any man be in Christ, he is a new creature: old things are passed away; behold, all things are become new. And all things are of God, who has reconciled us to himself by Jesus Christ, and has given to us the ministry of reconciliation; To wit, that God was in Christ, reconciling the world to himself, not imputing their trespasses to them; and has committed to us the word of reconciliation. **2 Corinthians 5:16-19**

The ministry of reconciliation has been entrusted to each one of us within the body of Christ. No member should suggest that they don't know what to do within the body. Soul winning is a responsibility for every believer; no one is too prominent to engage in winning souls for Jesus Christ. This duty is not reserved solely for the 'evangelism department of the church.' While it's beneficial to have evangelism teams, it is the responsibility of the entire body, including the pastor or leader of the assembly, to reach out and win the lost.

Following the guidance of the apostle Paul's admonition to Timothy, every minister of reconciliation must adhere to these guidelines.

I charge you in the presence of God and of Jesus Christ, who is to judge the living and the dead, and by his appearing and his kingdom: Preach the word; be ready on season and out of season; reprove, rebuke, and exhort, with complete patience and teaching. For the time is coming when people will not endure sound teaching, but having itching ears they will accumulate for themselves teachers to suit their own passions, and will turn away from listening to the truth and wander off into myths. As for you, always be sober-minded, endure suffering, **do the work of an evangelist**, *fulfill your ministry.* **2 Timothy 4:1-5**

We are called to 'always do the work of the evangelist' in season and out of season. Our ultimate endeavor, after being born again, is to judiciously engage in winning the lost.

Making excuses or shying away from reconciling people to God is simply not acceptable in God's kingdom because everything in the kingdom revolves around souls. God's love relates to souls, Christ's death, burial, and resurrection are because of souls, and the ministry of the Holy Spirit on earth is all about souls. If the Godhead holds the business of souls so dear, why are many Christians making excuses for not winning souls?

Our Responsibility

Understanding our fearful responsibility to the Lord, we work hard to persuade others. *God knows we are sincere, and I hope you know this too* (2 Corinthians 5:11 NLT).

We cannot afford to sit idly and watch people head down the road of destruction. We have received from the Lord the fearful responsibility to persuade and draw men to God. It won't be an easy task, as the devil will not watch them leave his kingdom without a fight. However, because we have received from the Lord this ministry of reconciliation, we must labor hard through prayers, intercession, soul winning, and evangelism for the lost.

The tactic of *'Go ye therefore into all the world'* must be forcefully employed by all believers of Jesus Christ, from the pulpit to the pews and in their various marketplaces or spheres of influence.

We must begin to go, meet, and engage the lost where they are, and stop waiting for them to come to us in our local assemblies. Christ didn't wait for us to come to God; He came to find us where we are and showed us the right way to the Father. We all must earnestly and fervently pray and act to stand true as ministers of reconciliation.

Love Claim

The true test of our love for God and people is to show people the right way – the way of salvation through Christ. We cannot claim we love God and not engage in His number one business, which is winning souls. Neither can we claim we truly love our neighbors if we refuse to show them the light or give up easily when they blatantly refuse the gospel of our Lord and Savior Jesus Christ. Love takes responsibility for others. *'For God so loved the world that He gave...'* (John 3:16).

God gave because He first loved. His gift of salvation and reconciliation through His Son was because He is love and loved the wicked world so dearly. Our love claim is only valid when we do as God did and is still doing – love and give.

Give your time in prayers for the lost. Give your time and resources to make sure they hear about the gospel. Persuade them with all your ability until they are convinced (by the power of the Holy Spirit working with us) that Jesus Christ is the only way to God.

God's Appeal

Since we are the light of the world and are called as ministers of reconciliation, God is making His appeal of salvation to the world through us. His desire is for us to make it our personal project to appeal to men everywhere and at all times to become saved. Don't wait until someone compels you to preach the gospel. Allow the compassion God has for souls to consume every fibre of your being. Everything you do in life must be because of souls. Whether you are a doctor, an artist, a lawyer – as long as you are born again, your job should only be a tool to do the work God has called you to do."

> *We are therefore Christ's ambassadors, as though God were making his appeal through us. We implore you on Christ's behalf: Be reconciled to God.* **2 Corinthians 5:20 (NIV)**

As ambassadors of Christ, we carry the responsibility to persuade people to be reconciled to God. I believe the world will respond positively to the gospel message we preach if we, as the sent ones, take the message seriously ourselves. We cannot afford to trivialize or underestimate the significance of the 'only message' that grants humans the life of God and eternal salvation. We must be thoroughly convinced of our identity as ministers of reconciliation and the message we bear. There is no other gospel approved by God that can save mankind; it is this very message for which Christ died

Practicalizing the Ministry of Reconciliation

We have affirmed that once our relationship with God is restored, we are individually called into His service—the service and ministry of reconciliation. Each one of us is commissioned by God to share the good news of His love, salvation, and peace with the world. Convincing people to enter into a reconciled relationship with God may seem daunting, especially in our post-modern society that respects moral decadence and often dismisses truth. To succeed, we must fully yield to the Holy Spirit, the Master Strategist in the harvest of souls. He is the Lord of the Harvest, and partnering with Him is essential, regardless of how challenging or impossible it may appear to win the lost. With the Holy Ghost, anyone can be won to Christ, regardless of their status or mindset, as long as we fervently pray, intercede for them, and allow the love of God to flow through us.

Many individuals out there are searching for the true message of reconciliation without even realizing it. It is our Christ-given responsibility to deliver this amazing life, destiny, and eternal gospel to them. Here are some ways to engage in the ministry of reconciliation:

1. Prayers, Intercessions, and Fasting

Continuous prayer and intercession for the lost, coupled with fasting, are vital components. Recognizing that the prayers of a righteous person avail much (James 5:16), the more we pray and intercede for the lost, the more we partner with the Holy Spirit in carrying out the ministry of reconciliation through us. Praying for the lost must be a continuous and deliberate act on our part as ministers of reconciliation.

2. Unity in Purpose

In these end times, the church must be unified to achieve the goal of winning the lost at all costs. We must come together as one, with the sole purpose of depopulating Hell. The era of internal strife must become a thing of the past. Embracing the mandate of collective and individual soul-winning as ambassadors of Christ is crucial. Apostle Paul emphasizes the importance of unity in purpose in the following verses of Scripture.

> *I planted the seed in your hearts, Apollos watered it, but it was God who made it grow. It's not important who does the planting, or who does the watering. What's important is that God makes the seed grow. The one who plants and the one who waters work together with the same purpose. And both will be rewarded for their own hard work. For we are both God's workers. And you are God's field. You are God's building.* **1 Corinthians 3:6-9(NLT)**

Our collective involvement in the pursuit of winning the lost should amplify our individual efforts. While someone or a group of believers may be praying and interceding for souls in one part of the world, someone else in another location may be preaching on the streets and winning souls as a result of those prayers. It doesn't matter who plants or waters the seed of the gospel; the most important Personality in this process is God, who makes the seed grow. Therefore, as long as we join hands – some planting and others watering – there is a guarantee of growth that will result in a mighty harvest, because the field belongs to God.

3. Soul Winning and Evangelism

Evangelism alone is not enough; we must take steps to win the souls we evangelize. Jesus instructed us to "*go and make disciples of all nations*" (Matthew 28:19).

Our calling is not just to go and tell but to go and make disciples. Soul winning is not solely the responsibility of evangelists or a selected few in the church; it is the duty of every child of God. The passion for winning the lost, coupled with intercessory prayers, will inevitably bring in the harvest.

There's a common phrase in the body of Christ that sometimes hinders the active engagement of believers in soul-winning efforts. The phrase, "It is the sheep that gives birth to the sheep and not the shepherd," is both wrong and ridiculous. It is against the gospel and God's mandate for souls. Every child of God, including leaders, is a sheep. In fact, leaders must lead the flock of God by example. Jesus, the Good Shepherd, led us by example.

4. Use all Means

Engage in the ministry of reconciliation using all the means available in our postmodern world today. While soul winning in the past relied heavily on crusades and one-on-one street evangelism, today we can reach more people quickly, both near and far, through various social media platforms and technology. The command to "go into the world" is a clarion call for the church to meet people where they are and not wait for them to come to the church. Without diluting the message of the gospel, we must present it rightly to the lost using all possible available means.

Conclusion: The Difference Makers

In conclusion, we are the difference-makers in the earth. God has prepared and equipped us for such a time as this, especially since we are in the end times. Every aspect of the ministry we are called into by the Lord must be taken seriously. We must be willing to give our all, even to the point of death. Despite the pressures around our daily lives, we must keep the Lord and His word as our focus. As the coming of our Lord draws nearer, Satan will intensify his attacks, positioning people in high places to pressure and persecute the saints. Some will openly deny their faith in Jesus Christ.

Don't be moved, child of God; stand your ground and represent who you are to the death. You may not be famous, and the world may not accept you as a true disciple of the Lord. But one thing is certain: our Master is with us, and He is greater than Satan and all hell combined. He has overcome the world. The church will begin to see a rise in the harvest of souls, and the Lord will move in the midst of His church, ushering in the manifestations of the sons of God. As we are in urgent times and seasons, we cannot afford to let down our guard for anyone or anything. The battle is on, but victory is already ours.

Many responsibilities hang on our shoulders, and we cannot afford to slack as difference-makers. Our words and deeds must portray the true Christ. The testimony of our faith must not be a reason for someone to reject or refuse the gospel of Christ but rather be a beacon of hope and faith in our God and in His Christ.

Someone out there needs to hear the word of the Lord from your mouth. Many lives are attached to yours that the Lord is counting on you to bring in.

Called and chosen ones, let's not disappoint the Lord and the saints who have gone before us. They passed the baton of responsibility for this gospel of love, grace, and mercy to us.

Then Peter said to Him, "Lord, do You speak this parable to us, or to all people?" And the Lord said, "Who then is that faithful and wise steward, whom his master will make ruler over his household, to give them their portion of food in due season? Blessed is that servant whom his master will find so doing when he comes. Truly, I say to you that he will make him ruler over all that he has. But if that servant says in his heart, 'My master is delaying his coming', and begins to beat the male and female servants, and to eat and drink and be drunk, the master of that servant will come on a day when he is not looking for him, and at an hour when he is not aware, and will cut him in two and appoint him his portion with the unbelievers. "And that servant who knew his master's will, and did not prepare himself or according to his will, shall be beaten with many stripes. But he who did not know, yet committed things deserving of stripes, shall be beaten with few. **"For everyone to whom much is given, from him much will be required; and to whom much has been committed, of him they will ask the more."** **Luke 12:41-48**

Anticipating Our Master's Return

Though He tarries, our Master will soon come with His reward in His hand (Rev. 22:12). Will He find you and me faithful in the ministry He has committed to us, or will He find us offering excuses for what we couldn't do for Him?

We've been given much; we've been called to make an impact and difference in this world, not by our own strength but by the working of the Spirit of God in and through us. Do you dare to make a difference? Do you dare to stand out even if you are standing alone? Will you be able to shun every form of compromise and work for your Master until you hear these words,

> *"...Well done thou good and faithful servant; you have been faithful over a few things, I will make you ruler over many things: enter into the joy of your Lord"* **Matthew 25:23**

www.ingramcontent.com/pod-product-compliance
Lightning Source LLC
LaVergne TN
LVHW052035080426
835513LV00018B/2334